GROOVE IS IN THE HEART

BY

JOEL WASHINGTON ATTERBURY

King Atterberry Ink

Copyrighted © 2021 Library of Congress.

Published by: Joel Washington Atterbury

ISBN: 978-1-7352952-2-0

Contact Information

Email: kingatterberry7@gmail.com

Facebook: Joel Washington Atterbury

Instagram: king_atterberry7

Instagram: king_atterberry_ink

Photographed submitted by Janice V Johnson

Memorable memory

Always I carry appreciation for my beautiful mother who brought me in this world.

Although she is not here in the physical, she lives through me along with my father.

HARLEM RAISED ME!!

&

SOUTH JERSEY EMBRACED ME!!

This book is dedicated to my mother

And

both of my great grandmothers

MRS. KAREN JALANEY HARRIS

Mrs. Lorraine Fitzgerald Washington

and

Mrs. Vinnie Wiggins Atterberry

TABLE OF CONTENTS

Just me

They keep on looking and searching for the author.

Lyrical enforcer caught ya who's your endorser.

Congratulations on what you see I'm on the other side.

Mystery rides capsize with no enterprise.

Keep playing around with king I do that other shit.

Sunduallah that's my nineties name no counterfeit.

I'm not hard to find I'm online like chat rooms.

See you real soon after you lose the attitude.

Fly as if they brought back the mike Tyson half-moon.

Always been justice league fighting legions of doom.

Sometimes you must shut down and wake back up.

Kill a bottle of champagne without getting stuck.

My luck is too advanced I'm a guard with no guardian.

Never liked partying just use to probably lobbying.

People get funny with moments like job meetings.

One group seating with different mindsets competing.

Get on your mark!!

Now or never has there been a poet born to
emcee.
Came from a school that kept students on
their left and right feet.
Hit the ground walk in ciphers with the ills of
thought.
Try not to get caught moving lines off
course.
Recite how you was taught be prepared for
the clowns.
So, if you spin their words around emotions
won't be found.
Hide your smile and load up from what you
have in the stash.
Go in your bag and grab some of the best
that you have.
Pen with skills of a barber and shoot like an
archer.

Come off the bench like a 6th man better than some starter.

No welcome back carter happy days is not what's happening.

If it's that time of the month go, get a coke and some aspirin.

Flow is like the 1st and 15th extra activity.

Still spit that poetry expressing lots of imagery.

Vividly get the picture painted when it's spoken.

Even if you read it there's emotion when it's open.

Let us begin

No need to push my pen I already been done that.

Different monikers on amazon check all facts.

I breathe on the laptop and kill the sleep mode.

Plagiarism on my ink y'all can keep those.

My sure shot decent some of y'all foul.

Take your ass to court witness a copyright trial.

Paper not even long my history strong.

My codependent always right while yours is wrong.

Four years of writing as a Titian I'm creative.

Got a style and cadence that microwave the haters.

Not the one to play with Reggie from the pacers.

When it's gone time, I am Lebron now with the Lakers.

From Harlem yes born and raised back in the day.

At the legal drinking age, I moved down to cape May.

Made a life had a kid had a wife became an author.

Even got a chance to hit the west coast border.

Before that hit Florida met some of my family.

Flew into Fort Lauderdale that's close to Miami.

Lantana where I stayed and had a nice piece of mind.

Nobody knows how I grind when I flow above the lines.

I'm nice!!

King!!

Too close!!

Coming from your direction that warm sweet
affection.

Makes our true grounded connection
illuminate our complexion.

The sound of your breathing while I'm feeling
your heartbeat.

Your back against my front as we touch each
other's feet.

My lips nibble on your earlobe and kiss u
with mystique.

Hands caress your thighs as my meat grow
on your cheeks.

However, our souls greet in this moment
passion confined.

No love is blind only smooth sailing hearing
the chimes.

Devoted as we promote the higher sensual
sides.

As our emotions collide sounding like water wave tides.

That commotion that was soaked in enhance our other chance.

Your beautiful ocean dance will have me waiting like the sand.

Always so beautiful while I am getting into you.

Mental trust first to highlight our time that's physical.

Afterward the visual as we continue to be spiritual.

Your all I need to proceed, and we don't have to be traditional.

Kiss your neck after I slightly bite you without your skin pierce.

This engineer appears and remain after the smoke clear.

Look inside your eyes and touch your lips with my fingertip.

Tongue inside your mouth while I tap you on your hips.

Slots

I'm getting chammy after chammy while I'm
hot on the slots.
My fiftieth birthday hot killing the slots with
no drops.
Told the machine build up my dough like
Texas hold.
Trigger fingers move fast as I go for more
dough.
Reinstated with the baker boys to make
noise.
I don't even have a choice to even express
my voice.
It's on and popping live life on what's
forgotten.
No holds barred I'm plotting pushing the limit
off my bargain.
Changing the rules law of the land kill
circumstance.

Spiritual side of me take a chance and start to chant.

I can't even hold back I gotta do what king do.

My crown spin around and shine bright like something new.

It's the pharmaceuticals and doctors cheating the elderly.

Life is not held properly they're on a state property.

Modern game monopoly some can't pass go.

Evil eyes can't hide from the truth they don't show.

Walk inside the unknown like I do knowing they spite you.

Never really like you front a smile mind is an ice cube.

Be like that now I don't breathe like that.

Leave that on trees that crack, branches deceased with sap.

Hold facts to the crap release that on cheesy rats.

Even the mice fall in a trap that's designed
for giant gnats.
Only clap I slap is finger snap poems and
raps.
I'm in love with all poetry forms and that's
that!

More than a flower

Just like a brand-new day with a brand-new feeling.

The most beautiful and bright in my sight so revealing.

Even the colors of what is can enlighten the coldest heart.

I would nickname her summer this time of year is the mark.

That is shown with a look of innocence at the same time precious.

A photo or even live visual is never helpless.

For what I see is amazing as I lay inside my patience.

Only time will be fine if she doesn't leave my motivation.

My mic is nice!

My mic is invisible when I am writing with a
pencil.
Without much potential on thoughts
becoming vengeful.
Either it's been a long time or levels to climb.
Always stay reclined with mines passing
time.
Soon as I feel a vibe and a sign is shown to
me.
The experience is found with another sharp
delivery.
Now that I'm half a century my mic shine
differently.
Futuristic energy downloaded to my memory.
The cord is more than explored before I saw.
An opportunity to left hand the mic and get
raw.
Science and evolution changing becoming
wireless.
Room become a fire pit bar or high as I can
get.

Intro the outro!

Bars are weak the flow is not accurate.

What you feel is passionate I don't think is adequate.

King smash through bull, as I rap my movement.

Always built off repetitive grooming salute influences.

Whether top five whether dead or alive.

There are levels to this no need to question why.

Swim inside the ocean of dreams enter reality.

Never had writers block that's made-up fantasy.

Angels dance with me from within to cleanse my sin.

Hoping to grab gods' attention and begin my life again.

Rise to the occasion be amazing I'm not playing.

Traitors be hating and waiting while perpetrating.

A fraud might be small but stand tall with instigators.

Next time my flavor layered with power from the creator.

Young judo!

Peep the all-white Hyundai returning home
on Sunday.
My apologies to Monday had to work back in
cape May.
Been a minute inside the molded stale air
facility.
Never will I be free from those who kill my
energy.
My presence opens doors of old mentality's.
No need for casualties switch up dark
polarities.
Only master me it's a king thing from the
family.
When the spirits enter me, I'm defeating most
of the enemy.
Pen game official OG's cosigned the juggler.
One helluva of a fella offset the troubled
suckers.
Only eyes that see and believe it's all visual.
The third sight ignite my only flight of all I
been through!

Play as we lay

Whether it's after the love or before the intimacy.
As she is touching herself, I stroke my myself gently.
This is that freaky sugar love that come from out the cut.
Her head laying across my upper leg but not to suck.
Looking me in my eyes giving me signs that she is pleased.
Opening ecstasy about the foreplay of our need.
I like the kiss she gave my leg as she is cuffing on my balls.
My soldier standing tall as my finger enter her hall.
Rubbing against her walls as I point tip to her face.

She gave a peck and said hold tight so that she can taste.

My heart starting to race as she watch enjoying time.

Moment about to climb the highest drive to give her mine.

As she receives a drink from king from his royalty stream.

Almost lost my whole mind in this reality scene.

This feign might be extreme like a pornographic screen.

But as we play as we lay it's just queen and a king.

Who knew pt.3

The ride keeps a beautiful view down on beach drive.

When I push it outside of its normal gaze its baptized.

Sunny in the county rays of light coat the vehicle.

Feeling so majestic I call my car imperial.

My physical monumental at a place that is essential.

Waves on the beach shore captivate my mental.

Fool proof my days of being housed its whatever.

These days are not better my study time is severed.

Balance the me time scales of worry don't hurry.

Remarkable comeback I'm lucky they didn't bury.

Thoughts of a rapport that wasn't lost or crossed.
At any restaurant tip the waiter after the course.
Main desert is a sweet thing creeping weekend.
Spiritual side of king take vacation without seeking.
Dreams of progress is the only thing honest.
Many times I wish like the song by carl Thomas.

Must I use it!

When I was young, I use to chill on the block
and spit bars.
Checking out the neighborhood superstars in
cars.
Sound system bumping the jams we love to
hear.
Beautiful young women walking by in tight
gear.
Nice round piece of a treat inside they dress.
Brothers looking hard almost losing they
breath.
On that timeline is when I started to rhyme.
We learned to design our lines inside our
minds.
Spit words ferocious poetry formed with
voltage.
Teamed with emcee soldiers charged with
high doses.

Writing and reciting was clever against whoever.

Crowds gathered around the cipher seeing who better.

Nice off the head yet still just an amateur.

Back then my bald head favored ken Bannister.

Whatever shots thrown competition made it known.

My poetry explodes from raps to written poems.

Ideas are clear when I appear and spit.

From an era where anyone can get what they get.

Don't challenge my pen game I do it by myself.

Whether typing or writing done by nobody else.

The mentor for me is a spiritual consciousness.

Raise king a compliment it's all written with confidence.

What it is

The world is compromised between the
poison in the sky.
Now that the land is feeling dry some can see
the earth cry.
There's a dilemma inside the center where
lab test is born.
Oaths are being taken on old bible that's
worn.
Now that society is masked my view inside of
a glass.
Population controls check the gauges on the
graph.
Citizen opinions been global and unclear.
What they threw inside the air is totally
engineered.
What we fear is an enemy shit just offended
me.
My distilled energy is built from a
community.

Love inside a conscious of blood inside my physical.

Fight against a world that might wanna get rid of you.

Protect what's left never project stories that's guessed.

Isolation through patience my day of rest is flexed.

Hydrate on a good one drink fast upon the outcome.

Don't contemplate the problems elevate from the bottom.

Before and after

Never mind what they heard come see who is here.

It's the king without a crown making everything clear.

I'm so sincere when I appear in the moment.

Making favorites get out voted by the underdog opponent.

Prepare things naturally bring your A game properly.

Make sure you don't copy me this verse is a robbery.

Stand like an adventure when the fight is all over.

Change your old motor I'm a spitter and a soldier.

Keep everything decent up to par with what's recent.

Whatever I release quick I'm always at peace with.

They say the brainwaves activate and trigger
your thoughts.
Whoever said I'm soft better double check
the source.
Too many get batteries thrown in the
backpacks.
Find yourself left back searching for Aflac.
In the end getting laughed at the stage is a
small set.
This ain't even my best work proceeds
without caution.

Open delivery

I see the world through a paranormal lens
nothing but entities.
The challenge of protecting another side of
me is killing me.
Days becoming harder every physical being
is different.
How can I distinguish the difference without
being a witness?
My story unfolds living inside an episode.
What television show am I casted to play a
role.
Focusing myself on the reflection in the
mirror.
Somethings becoming clearer hopefully I'm
not in fear of.
Illness of society the world is full of
troublemakers.
Reminiscing on time before smart phones we
had pagers.

So many lost in thought of what is or supposed to be.

Social media changing human beings' identities.

Filters and blasphemous post ghosting the realness.

Bring back the builders of knowledge of self and kill this.

Destructive mindset let's collect a group of teamsters.

Copacetic dreamers and pure the heart cleaners.

Let's breathe

My day just beginning with an athletic
breakfast.
Toast poached eggs with orange juice no
effort.
Take full vitamins while lifting while I'm
listening.
To motivational speakers while I'm steady
getting in.
Squats and curls a few stretches and some
climbers.
At half a century I'm trying to unlock my
blinders.
Keep my mind sharper than pencils hitting
loose leaf.
I'm at my highest peak while some stay
underneath.
True time of belief power of now is in the
present.

Must stop second guessing about unanswered questions.
Benevolent blessings acquired soon as we transform.
To a higher mental form that's why I crossed my left arm.
Science in and out the books I learned from others.
Maintain your righteous life always rock with those who love ya.
Many prayers to their goals get out the Peter rabbit hole.
One day they'll understand king Atterbury 'Soul.

FREESTYLE PT.1

They wanna sleep on the no doze I'm cold in
all seasons.

Forget king atterberry my ink still bleeding.

Whichever way you want it there will never
be comfort.

Whatever you take from it make you sick to
your stomach.

Pack a meal and a half I have a can for your
trash.

Right hand of the flash my hulk and thing
crash your path.

Sunduallah only return to make sure you join
the worms.

No need to be concerned dead heads about
to learn.

Why your tomb so consumed by the others
in the room.

They just waiting they turn for my third eye to
zoom.

Bring your whole crew aura watch I turn into a porter.

Clean and clear the area up here's to all the mourners.

A program explaining why and how they took the shots.

It was a black lightning shock dropping them cowards in the spot.

Spin off to the next location for those waiting.

It doesn't take long creating my pen and pad always mating

Off switch

When I pull out that heatwave the temperature is solar.

Wake up the sleeping soldiers I call this flow Folgers.

My combats raps sound like a forty-five busting.

The competitor is back so let's drop empty discussions.

I still hear the whispers as I stare at my pops picture.

Drinking that dark liquor seeing his face in sink mirrors.

My thoughts aren't tainted I'm only maintaining.

Only thing I don't understand is what people claiming.

These bars become flagrant swinging full violation.

Better watch what you're facing before I turn into Jason.

The stroll is quicker than the sneak steps of a feign.

Who lost his last hit now searching for Scottie's beam?

Mentally a pupil of Spock reading his literature.

Vulcan style test me now watch you grow a weird frown.

Some wish I suffer from the instance of a dark cloud.

End of day I'm black and proud y'all Franks with extra sauerkraut.

MJY!

A lot been going on since my mother passed on.

Moved to south Jersey where things were out of norm.

Salt is in the air so I'm breathing sort of differently.

Not many know my history that's probably why they shifty.

Coming from a time where brothers dropped knowledge.

My people stood they ground with hard strengthened cartilage.

Built my home in cape may raise daughters and sons.

It's a whole different world from the Harlem slums.

Had to change ways of thinking a whole new beginning.

At twenty one left polluted skies to the forbidden.

County in this new state new place mixed race.

Moving around at a cool pace love gave me new taste.

Dived into employment kitchen work serving tables.

At home my television was rigged without cable.

Silver bullet in the back of the set pray on connection.

If the reception of a signal came in it was a blessing.

JW PT.2

Very thankful for the bloodline that run in my genes.

My father's father left a spiritual message in my dreams.

Started out on a journey through a DNA site.

Found matches that activated my inner eyesight.

Many clues to choose and use connecting dots.

Enter pieces inside of a puzzle that was a lot.

Nah

As months and years ran by caught different hits.

The magnificent rapport with matches gave me a list.

Through god I gained spiritual ways to be a tracker.

Then next what came after a spectacular factor.

Now I got to see what was believed off someone's tree.
Helping me find out about my family ancestry.
Conversations here and there greatly appeared.
Feeling like Alex Hailey with roots my chandelier.
Held light that shine bright more than time before.
More family came about in my life with love to pour.
The significance of seeing the radiance of discovery.
The creator is above me and keeping me good company.

Better Recognize 20/21

Ain't nothing but a small thing to get up in the ring.

Your application for destruction is filed on both wings.

Wanna get fly talk slick and get greasy.

Believe me I choke others out with no memory.

Walk off as if nothing happened body a problem.

Found next to an entrance that said already bombed him.

No need to calm the drifter there's already a mix up.

Comedians and tricksters, I'm still a quick spitter.

Write as if big red signed me under false shit.

If I was in deep water still would off a dolphin.

My offering to the sea world this is how I see world.

Crush mamas pearl feed his chick until she URL.

Touch planet from Atlantic with havoc while others panic.

This is titanic and gigantic because they challenge.

It's ugly stop rambling whoever feel they are challenging.

This is big man moment go and call your management.

No need to squash what already been resolved.

Next time you might get washed and found in a garage.

No door closed we want you fully exposed.

Like a housewife on a corner and her husband didn't know.

So, peep it this that gritty from the city blip.

This is only half a clip without no loose music.

Taken for granted

Only ones that see it coming are the true born seekers.

Hear the word from the speakers of leaders that are featured.

Accommodations made when you engage in what they say.

There's no time to play where we live it's not safe.

Too much politics on the laws passed and changing.

Next level gaming we need futuristic training.

Backs need watching our minds need better learning.

Flip a coin on what's turning as the sun keep burning.

Earth need assistance what happened to the fighters.

Probably being held back by government liars.

Paperwork lost in a system that's still damaged.

Big brother got cameras connected to global scanners.

Downloaded in my physical is a deep version of manners.

Soon as I hang a banner projected with new grammar.

It won't take a toll on forces that are United.

Whether you hate or love it don't matter you will like it!

Full notice

These cyanide lyrics hope it touch the
unrighteous.
Too much conversation with the highest of
the flyers.
Meaning the ones who run from an
orchestrated plan.
Unfortunately, the man caught someone with
gun in hand.
This is bars behind bars war wounds from a
prisoner.
Making sure it reaches those who was with
the spinners.
Tales told ice cold what happened to the
right folks.
Changed into the light coat before the winter
mouth close.
Loyalty is suspect that's why sometimes
we're upset.

Neglect of respect is so direct that snitches break sweat.

When a name drops, and their situation brought up.

Eyes give it all up they caught up and emotionally tore up.

Prayers for our people that are equal to our own life.

Never pass judgement watch them others with the hot dice.

Wicked as a poltergeist inside a world of darkness.

Throw something on the commissary for our prisoned artist.

Stamped!!

Let's get straight to it this that fluid music.

Show you how to do it watch how king rule it.

It's wild outside for these mothers of kids.

Crazy how they be tricking for dollars in cribs.

Shame how they move just to bust a move.

Can't judge what they do it's an old groove.

The guard only speaking what he knows about.

They at the fella house while his wife is out.

Such a nice chick but lost in the world.

Mamas baby girl got the game fucked up.

How do we teach the youth with the show and prove?

Some already lost trapped inside they attitude.

Kids raising kids that's another story.

Inside and outside where is god's glory.

You can always free your mind for divine acceptance.

Join a choice of efforts to obtain your blessing.

Change the dusty road find a better goal.

Get off that hoe stroll you already know.

Confused and consumed by the street life.

Bring that sacrifice correct the wrong with the right.

I'm just a narrator who have seen it all.

Even though we all fall but get back up and find a door.

Open and enter ground your thought inside the center.

One day remember this was presented by ninja!

You!

Nice bottle of wine that's chilled before the meal.

Small period of time to kill speak and reveal.

About how we feel on life and try to capture.

Moments of expression between minutes of laughter.

Although your easy on the eyes but what lies inside.

Can we form a good connection with a telepathic vibe?

Give rapport a try gifts a ribbon from the sky.

If getting close to you is a crime, I want no alibi.

Lock me up inside your heart and hide the key.

Embrace me in your life as if you just found your chi.

Vibrant energy that's dispersed from gods' house.

Believe I'm on a path that's close to all your routes.

My intuition strong only fueled by gods' angels.

The same ones that came to you made me thoughtful.

First time I saw you looking sweet, kind and adorable.

Knew I had to find a better way to make this audible.

Good morning, good evening!!

No stranger to pots and pans I'm the man behind the hands.

Step inside the kitchen cooking my intuition unplanned.

Recipe for love carry no prime ingredients.

If you see me in the light its always shining medium.

Sweet lady I got it covered knowing your gonna love it.

Utilizing all utensils and things from out your cupboard.

Allow the food to cook slow while I touch your soul slow.

By the way my name is joel can I kiss your hidden flow.

Rub your neck to open codes just to see inside your fold.

Let me get back to the food making sure it's good to go.

After the grub check with objects, I'm walking to you next.

Place my lips upon yours I appreciate the peck.

Pour two glasses of wine and prepare plates of care.

Just beware I'm only being sincere enjoy my air.

This moment is beautiful read my eyes there's no disguise.

As I live inside the high because I'm that type of guy!

Follow tomorrow

From out the house of L, location at the shore.
Cruise around the county as if I paid for town tours.
Shorts and shirt matching Air ones hold my feet.
No socks on the dock my spot open for weeks.
Clean looking sheik all white angel apparel.
Only image after me is my physical self-shadowed.
Nothing is wrong I feel reborn reading psalms.
My demons are gone the creator keeping me strong.
Temptation and fear are in the past so now I laugh.
I'm on a path that is longer than a neck on giraffe.

Been waiting for this moment to end my hard struggle.

To myself I'm saying Blackman rumble Blackman rumble.

So, to the ropes in the world that have a ring to hold me in

I am determined to reach my goal and get far until the end.

Manifest dreams on a scale larger than life.

Next time I scribe a poem I'm gonna let it take flight.

I'm gone!

Bring it back

Although the time now so much is foul and
wild.
When I turn the dial check out the sound I
found.
To understand how is to know the guard.
Spoken word to crowds leaving a mental
mark.
Adjust thoughts of theory hoping some can
hear me.
Lost is many states fighting against a fury.
Land of confusion too much extra in the
memo.
Change and refocus can this all be so simple.
Nothing strange just an upgrade on the
download.
We live inside a place to control our
household.
Jobs are cutting hours while they raising up
a tower

Rebuild a tower they turning sweet hearts to sour.

Strong arms weakening losing strength to keep form.

Stress on the physical and mental positions torn.

Predicted many years ago perhaps we didn't know.

Nowadays it's no joke grab prosperity and grow.

Your welcome

As I walk into whatever it is, suppose to be.

Experience, occurrences learn about the new me.

True understanding while opening the curtains.

My purpose so big right now my past is hurting.

What I make to happen bring the heart of the strong.

Tear up the form that belong to the old me that's gone.

Listen to old songs feel the tunes in the ear.

There was a time that existed but now disappeared.

Lift the spirit from the bottom to remain on top.

If my physical stop I'll coexist with my pops.

Allow my kids motivation to inspire me to live.

Embrace the growth that's close hope in all faith I kiss.

Proud of new ways to engage every day.

Turn skies dark and grey to a beautiful display.

Bright life so colorful through the lights of god.

Utilize my smarts to learn from studies that were hard.

The enemy lurking when confusion is on the rise.

How about we take a ride inside of gods holy skies.

Move accordingly in the world without a doubt internal.

Never worry about the informal gestures they don't concern you.

SPECIAL SHOUT OUT TO MY
BROTHERS AND SISTERS IN POETRY:

Poetic Meadows, Jrob The Wise Son

Mojavi Emi, For-real the poet Douglass

Brian Donnell, Aaron R. Whitehead

Anita Manning, Nicole R. Brookins

Donyelle Chaney, Adrienne Showell

Gena Storm, T La Shalle

Jazzi Skye, Whitni Wells

Edwina Simmons, Rita Simmons

Jarrod King, Nicole Teardrop Williams

Kamal Imani, Safiyyah Amina1389

Also, peace and love to Govan

Cousins:

Marva Rodgers, Alana brown, April Williams, Tonia Mckoy

And now to my beautiful cousin who grace the cover of this book:

Mrs. Janice V. Johnson thank you for allowing me to use your image on my last poetry project of the year.

I would like to thank everyone that have supported me by purchasing my books.

Also, a big thank you to my tribe that keep me alive doing what I do and keeping me inspired and motivated.

Check out the poetry corner show!!

"PEACE AND LOVE"

KING ATTERBERRY

THIS BOOK WAS SPIRITED BY MY FATHER:

JOEL WASHINGTON ATTERBURY SR.

WHO PASSED AWAY AT THE AGE OF 32!

SLEEP IN PEACE DAD!!

I love and miss you!!

www.ingramcontent.com/pod-product-compliance
Lightning Source LLC
Chambersburg PA
CBHW071223170626
46809CB00005BA/1912